# POETRY BIRMINGHAM

# POETRY BIRMINGHAM
## *Literary Journal*

Autumn 2019 — Issue One

EDITORS

*Suna Afshan*
*Naush Sabah*

PALLINA PRESS LIMITED.
BIRMINGHAM

# POETRY BIRMINGHAM
*Literary Journal*

Pallina Press Limited, Birmingham
www.pallinapress.com

Typeset & Design:  Suna Afshan, Adrian B. Earle, and Naush Sabah

ISSN 2633-0822
ISBN 9781686641824

## COVER IMAGE

Holy Grail Tapestry – Quest for the Holy Grail Tapestries – Panel 6 – The Attainment;
The Vision of the Holy Grail to Sir Galahad, Sir Bors, and Sir Percival
Commissioned in 1895 by Laurence Hodson for Compton Hall near Wolverhampton;
Based on Le Morte d'Arthur by Sir Thomas Malory
Designed by Sir Edward Burne-Jones, William Morris, and John Henry Dearle
Manufactured by Morris & Co, 1907
Photo by Birmingham Museums Trust, licensed under Creative Commons CC0

Birmingham
Museums

## SUBMISSIONS

For our guidelines visit www.poetrybirmingham.com

Submission windows:
1st to 31st March
1st to 30th June
1st to 30th September
1st to 31st December

I will now no longer hide me from you, but ye shall see
now a part of my secrets and of my hidden things . . .

*Le Morte d'Arthur*, Sir Thomas Malory

Nature never set forth the earth in so rich
Tapestry as divers Poets have done . . .

*The Defence of Poesy*, Sir Philip Sidney

I am not yet finished, and he looked at the pages before him—
the music still falling from them.

'The Maestro', Hisham Bustani
translated by Thoraya El-Rayyes

# Contents

# EDITORIAL

*Suna Afshan • Naush Sabah*

Soundtrack: 'Four Sea Interludes' from *Peter Grimes*, Benjamin Britten

Currite ducentes subtegmina, currite, fusi.

*Poem 64*, Catullus

We lay our spread of white paper on a table at the Parkside building and pause in the cathedralesque silence of its atrium. Like the expectant mothers of Faustine Ladeiro-Levent's opening poem, we have met by the canalside and waited for the flood. Now, on a balmy summer evening, it's time to draw out the natural order of the poems which comprise this inaugural issue of *Poetry Birmingham* and we 'stand knee-deep, trying to snatch sound or significance,' like Michelle Penn's water-reader. Having moved from the punctuation mark, the single word, the line—where it extends, draws itself taut, breaks—to the stanza and its flocking into shape, we've come *finally* to the whole, and to the words of our first editorial.

In the 1980 January–February issue of *PN Review*, the late Donald Davie wrote:

> One has seen it so often before: the professed and often enough sincere wish to *purify* poetry—to purify it of politics, of logic, of intentionality behind the poetic utterance, and consequently of any responsibility

on the poet for what he utters. Always the overt intention is to exalt poetry; and always the effect is to emasculate it. A poetry that demands these freedoms will in our society be granted them. Thus purified, thus *purged*, poetry does neither harm nor good; it can safely be ignored, compassionately tolerated, contemptuously complimented. Poetry's enemies, and poetry's false friends, ask nothing better. Poetry conceived of in this way will count for nothing in our corporate life; and it deserves to count for nothing.

Strains of this observation have cropped up in conversation between us for years now—this wider discourse on poetry's purpose, a moth encircling candlelight, throwing itself against an artificial sun, becoming finer than even ash. To question one's ontology is human. It's an undeniable marker of cognisance, of intelligence; the poetry we have always been drawn to as individuals and now as editors seems to ask that question of itself: 'Why,' it says, albeit a little melodramatically, 'must I exist?' This journal exists because it must. It exists because we have spent too long in repurposed smoking rooms, wondering why there's a poetry-journal-shaped hole in Birmingham's cultural footprint.

Both of us delight in our city: in its green spaces and waterways, its inner-city bustle and suburban quietude, its high streets and intermingled university campuses, the timbre of jazz that spills out of coffeehouse doorways, in the art dotted around us, in its wealth of poetry nights. It is a city rich in literary heritage and culture; engaged in contemporary poetry through thriving open mics, literature festivals, and small presses. Our cover image is a tapestry held in the collection at Birmingham Museum and Art Gallery—a twenty-minute walk from where we congregate to read and breathe our poetry—like C. S. Lewis' wardrobe, it's a portal into the literary tradition we stake a claim in and endeavour to augment with the publication of *Poetry Birmingham*.

The misguided wish to purify poetry may in effect neuter it. However, that wish being articulated allows Davie to make the argument for poetry that 'traffics in realities' including the political, and for us to continue that discourse today. To stay with the *PN Review*, in this year's March–April issue Michael Schmidt cites one editor's suggestion of substituting the word 'silence' for 'deafness' in a poem and refers to it as an 'unravelling of texture' and an erasure which the reader will remain unaware of in the published text. This is perhaps an instance of politics neutering the poem. One wonders why a poet would agree to a change if indeed it is a matter of erasure and unravelling and not simply an exercise in seeking the right word. In any case, Schmidt's comment means that readers are now aware. Poets no more wish their palimpsests published than editors do and editing has to stop before the integrity of the poem is lost between drafts. That may mean a poem needs to find an alternate home; an editor needs to find another poem for her pages. It may mean that editors publish something they would still further change if they could, or poets concede where they feel they shouldn't have. For some of us, the business remains unfinished. But it ought to be possible to open the door to readers and allow them to eavesdrop or interject in these discussions.

A journal with more than one editor is a creative collaboration but more importantly an ongoing dialogue and negotiation with one another, our poets and our readers. This requires more than an editorial. It requires meetings over coffee and long discussions after poetry nights. It requires panels and Q&As. It requires emails back and forth or even tweets. It requires essays and reviews—which we intend to introduce in subsequent issues, and welcome pitches and submissions for. We invite our readers to respond, and leave space at the back of the journal for you to do so, be it through poetry or comment.

This summer, the weather turned from polite conversation filler to cause of deep-seated dread, and those anxieties weave through the tapestry of this issue. Its warp is violence and art, and its weft is nature and change. There is the ever-present nostalgia of childhood, and fractures which cut through those memories like 'lead shot', to borrow from Alix Scott-Martin's striking image. Defiant daughters transmogrify into wolves or watchful guards. It brings to our minds not only the transnatural and uncanny, but also the defiance of girls like Greta Thunberg and her attempt to shake the politics of the present by the shoulders. Her actions, indeed, the whole Extinction Rebellion movement, seem of almost Biblical import: 'And a little child shall lead them.' Or perhaps, like blind believers, like the millennial optimists we are, we abandon all logic for hope.

We might surmise that the kids are alright. 'Men,' however, 'may need our help,' says Mark Russell, and his prose poem asks directly: 'If war is a distinguishing characteristic of human nature, how might we explain the existence of music?' This is a juxtaposition that Phil Miller's 'Britten at Belsen' explores at length as it confronts the consequences of fascism. In Serena Trowbridge's poem, music allows 'fine tracing tendrils [to] creep across the aisles', to 'stretch up and stroke the heavens.' It's tantalising to see art as a means of ascension or bridging divides, but impossible to indulge in the thought for too long when Ian Dudley's 'Ironmaster' reminds us of the human cost of art and architecture and John Porter's 'The Council' makes much besides bureaucracy seem ridiculous in the face of the impending climate catastrophe.

And poetry, so obsessed with its own genesis—an editorial, so obsessed with its own genesis—is always aware of its mortality. The chalice before us, the hundred pages in your hands, will serve to bind this publication within the fabric of this city and this tradition, no matter how frail and inconsequential the new thread may seem to us now. We are joining a long line of individuals who, in their role as poetry editors, have functioned to uphold a responsibility to lyric and her living tradition; a duty to curate journal issues which illustrate the vitality of poetry today and the robustness of its criticism. We are willing to take risks in order to foster ambitious prosody and provide space for the considered critical attention one must bring to the art of poetry. We hope you find both pleasure and provocation within the pages of *Poetry Birmingham*.

## FAUSTINE LADEIRO-LEVENT

## Before the War Ends

We give birth slick and frog-legged.
Our waters meet by the riverbank
as we wait for the flood, gooey-eyed,
sticky, our ankles thick like eels.

We crouch like animals and swallow
the ginger-heat of the desert with barren throats,
our last meal of bread and beer sediment on our tongues,
the cornerstones of labour in our grip.

One hundred settlements collapse in the sand.
Husbands locusts in warpaint; the world spirals
into ochres as they run to the river, feed
on its flower, drain the water from its mud.

We build amphibious children, element-shifters
wailing through liquid and dust,
their bodies on our bodies like clay.
We carve statues of ourselves,

contortionists made beggars,
and as we pray to idols in the shape of cows we wish
we were the hyenas laughing at the blue sun.
Our babies will be born with teeth.

# SERENA TROWBRIDGE

## Green Music

A formal hush arises. The audience sit neatly
in box-hedge rows, expectancy dulled by experience.
Some think of where else they might be. Muttering
silence rolls on like muffled thunder in stormy trees.

A man enters with a fiddle, leaping on the stage.
His eyes are algae-bright like frogs, or lichen,
and their gaze is wetly piercing. A rustling applause,
thin and mean, scatters as he lifts his violin, darts the bow
and scrapes—

the words tumble, speaking a Babel blast
the people feel they've heard before
ánd as he plays, the great hall

       shifts. The limelight flows, fine tracing tendrils
creep across the aisles, o the green leaves grow—

and glow, brighter sharper faster. The words
of the fiddle fall to the floor to form a hill
and over it grows grass, and the audience is moved
but still afraid, uncertain. Bindweed winds
around their ankles, while they listen agape, aghast.

Silently words fall from their mouths becoming
flowers, daisy chains linking them together
as the word mountain cracks open, erupting, spewing
clouds of viridian foliage. There are no words

for this luxuriance; language is leaving them,
flying through the opening roof towards an
avocado sky, which pours in to meet

the leaves, the trees of words, the notes—
sound which stretches up to stroke the heavens.
A mossy light deepens, darkens. In the olive
gloom the people sprout new, fresh

growth of twigs and buds, while the music
—no melody ever heard was like this, and they
dance, admiring their leafy extremities

o the green the greenness of life of trees of fingers—
                              The fiddler stops.
The sky recedes, verdurous leaves wither and turn
to brown; the light is brighter, artificial, yellow.

The audience is returned, clap dutifully, and slip
out in silence to a world of cars and televisions,
chip shops and factories. Dead leaves remain.

# ALIX SCOTT-MARTIN

## Sometime Daughter

*She that herself will sliver and disbranch*
*From her material sap, perforce must wither*
*And come to deadly use.*
King Lear IV.ii.

Early morning, I follow you into the forest—
you and your men and your dogs,
gun slung over your shoulder. Old man,
you have grown so stooped.

If I announce my love to the earth, now,
it will sound like boots on dead leaves.
We both know it can't grow roots,
not in mud, rutted hard with frost,
glittering in slices of November light.

So I trail behind and open my mouth like a yawn or a scream,
billow my breath into the shadows—
smoke from a bonfire, from your pipe.

Up ahead, you bend slowly to pick up a stick, wrist-thick,
you turn and wield it like a baton,
tell me to take it.

I beat the bare trees like a drum, sullenly thwack their rough bark.
They answer with an outburst of wings and a stupid squawk.
You lift the barrel as though you were hinged at the waist
and shatter the sky.

A gift from the gods plummets and thumps into ferns
for spaniels that sit and fetch like daughters,
while the forest regathers a silence.

I carry your killings, of course, with their floppy necks
and blood on my gloves.
They are still warm in gilded feathers,
jade-capped, eyes bright and blind as holly berries,
soft as girls' hair if you hold their breasts to your cheek.

Crows flap and chatter in the branches
above where you sit hunched on a tree stump, dead birds on your lap,
plucked clean, flesh like jaundiced babies.

You have cut off their heads and pushed your fingers deep inside,
pulled out guts which gleam and stink and steam,
kidneys, a liver, a heart like a tiny balled fist.

When the rain comes, it drops like tears.
Imagine if it fell hot as my scorn, it would sear furrows into your cheeks.


We sit at a vast table,
you at the far end, distant as a snow-covered field,
expecting to be served.

I grip the little bones in my fingers, tear at them with my teeth,
wolf-hungry, until juices run down my chin.
I meet your eye, spit lead shot hard onto my plate.

# ELLORA SUTTON

## I Became the Wolf

Something about a wicker basket,
neatly padded with chintz and brimming
with rosemary bread, a thermos of soup,
a tome of cheese and a card I'd made myself
with blunt felt-tips, the paper folded,
all uneven. *Get Well Soon.*

Maybe I skipped at first, or at least
held a spring in my step, singing girlishly
to the daffodils and baby's breath.
The first green was cathedralesque,
dragonflies and maidenhair ferns, wet
with the gleam of fecundity. The psalms
were babbled and breezy. I learnt them, easy.

I learnt them all. Doc leaves for stings,
the correct way to suck the tough skin
of holly to tea, how to dodge dog shit.
The road was longer than I remembered
and lit only by the sharp silver wick of birches
like lunar nail-clippings. I followed the path
until there was no path. I followed

the notches in Orion's belt, undid
my mildewed red hood and howled.
I was just a kid, little girl lost
in the woods under the stars, lost
on the way to her grandmother's house.

It must have been my eyes. The fish
swam straight into my hands, the rabbits
offered their necks for dandelions. Birds
made themselves known by their glassy songs,
their eggs left blind in the basket. Berries
bloodstained my teeth, my tongue, the green
became violence. The green trickled down my spine
like red trickled down my chin.
A girl, by nature, is a wild thing.

Still I walked. My feet turned to dirt;
I licked them clean. My palms turned to leather,
my knees to crossbow triggers. Poised,
I bled freely. I fed on the night air and
sun-honey, gobbled all the soft little white things
that offered themselves to me. My cape, embroidered
with rosehips and cow parsley, choked
around my throat with its crimson ribbon.
I didn't realise how I'd grown. I shed it,
the way I'd seen snakes shed their skin.

There was something I could remember,
from before the wood. A big old book
about a woman naked in a forest
with an apple and a fig leaf. Tell me—
did she ever feel this free?

# Coven/Transfiguration

We snap their ribs. Milkish things.
Cloister rubble and crush.
Break bones for marrow.

It is flaxen hot, this summer.
Thatch our hair into fields,
we lay.
Parch and pucker.

How the heather goes up.
Seed to whisper, to flame
to uncontrollable blaze.
Rage is a bruise or a graze.

Gut the foetus of a fig.
Wasp-sting and swallow.
Our samplers are saturated,
beaded with pomegranate seeds.

We skin hares for their eyes
and feet. Honest blood on our chins,
we run.
The love is violet strong.

We writhe in the dirt. Germinate.
Beg for the burs of each other.
We are becoming and
become.

Burn blaze burn.
Volition and choice,
the fire is honey, is sugar,
disintegrating us to dust.
They can't tell one from the other.

# To Myself at 16
*a Golden Shovel after Marty McConnell*

Girl, you need to learn how to take.
Just take. Don't give a shit. Don't give a
fuck. Take. Sunflowers, bones, a lover,
driftwood. They won't listen. Who?
The world. Ignore their aniseed looks.
You are made of cardamom and dirt; at
worst you are a forest. At best? Look at you,
rottweiler, dragon, high priestess. Soft like
a mushroom cloud. Forget about maybe.
Remember your mother; she had teeth, and you,
a spat canine. Your fists are nettles are
smashed glass, glittering with blood, not magic.

# Note

The world outside my bedroom window is one of total greenness. Looking out at it right now I can see birds, branches heavy with red berries, drowsy fern fronds and, if I stretch my eyes, hills made violent with heather. This has been my view for all twenty-two years of my life, and it tends to seep into my writing

The forest is a place of transformation. In 'I Became the Wolf'—my retelling of Little Red Riding Hood—it is a liberating space, where the only thing that matters is survival. It allows Red to shed the choking hood of gentleness and vulnerability enforced by societal conventions around femininity. The forest offers a similar haven to the women in 'Coven/Transfiguration'. I love the idea of recasting women from traditional fairy/folktales. Little Red Riding Hood becomes the apex predator rather than the doe-eyed victim in need of rescue; just as the witches are no longer caricatures through whom female power is vilified but are simply, and unapologetically, powerful women. More than that, they are women who stick together, who love each other and refuse to suffer for it.

'To Myself at 16' is a Golden Shovel, which uses a line from Marty McConnell's spellbinding poem, 'Frida Kahlo to Mary McConnell'. Again, nature creeps in, although in a more abstract way. This is a more personal poem, and it's hard for me to write about myself without referencing the wilderness I grew up with. It is, I suppose, my way of trying to tell myself to be more like the character in 'I Became the Wolf'. To me, feminism is power. Nature, too, is power, and in my work the two themes are often inextricably entwined.

*Ellora Sutton*

CHRISTINA THATCHER

## Sentry

I was ready:
camping all those nights
on the living room floor, broken
door locks rattling. Ready for the ransacking,
the burn of bad people who'd let themselves in.
Ever watchful daughter, refusing fear,
my heartbeat slow as a funeral drum.
I was ready: *It's your job, house canary.*
*Just watch the door and call*
*if we need to run.*

# HILARY ROBINSON

## As If
*VII Thou shalt not commit adultery*

as if there was a wall
you could put up between
a promise and a honeymoon

as if a trench without
a bridge could
keep you safe

as if an *I do*
or two could guarantee
I would be all

# April 1997

That day I made it to the village.
At the doctors I listened
as she talked about the healing
benefit of a daily walk.
All I wanted was the pills
that cancel out rage and despair
like those half-remembered equations
I couldn't quite master in maths.

Walking home I saw a sale board
on a cottage. Small, stone, its door
right on the pavement. I didn't press
my nose to the window—couldn't
bring myself to leave a mark.
But I looked in. I saw a fireplace,
imagined flames, my birthday cards
on the mantlepiece, a polished floor,
soft rugs and dark red walls. Art.

Beyond the living room I guessed
at a kitchen with no soap splashed
up the window. There was a cat's bowl
by the back door and the smell of scones
fresh from the oven. My mixer and my apron
were both there. Upstairs, a terracotta quilt
and walls of gold with floor-length curtains,
a single pair of slippers by the bed.

The sun was shining or maybe
it was raining as I turned away.
Head down, I watched my feet
bring me home.

# Robert Selby

## One Poem *from* 'Chevening'

*III.*

Your tread around the ornamental lake
        was comically unsure,
                your pumps picking with balletic care
                        where to come down
                                among the green goose shit.

We swayed, arm in arm.
        We waited for the promised carp
                but saw only dull minnows
                        in black lanes through green algae
                                carved by a family of Greylag.

We stood before the purple door
        of an old wooden boathouse,
                providing a moonlight-divined
                        sanctum for illicit lovers,
                              or a murdered governess

scanning the water
        for her own reflection.
                We didn't enter,
                        retracing our steps beneath
                                the limes, the bubble-gum blossom.

# Rebecca Ruth Gould

## Restraint

In the Hungarian Pastry Shop,
lovers' favoured haunt,

your thumb grazes my fingers.
Your blue eyes linger. I don't resist.

As for the rest, I accept the limits:
children, wives, daily lives.

Coffee warms the fingers. Tiramisu teeters
on our plates like leaning towers of Pisa.

The crowd subsides.
Only dreamers haunt these nocturnes.

Although I long
for the touch of your lips,

I will not turn this moment
into a cliché

by feeding you tiramisu.
Instead, I will await the day

when age makes us sexless
& desire is a memory,

when thinking of you—
& thinking with you

—lingers longer than
the urge to kiss you.

# Leila Howl

## Diurnal

I get a day
to fill
the longings of a year.
Or longer.
Decades.
Since a lifetime of sunshine turned to snow
in a day—
from genetically engineered towns
to wind-rushed beaches. Ours, all winter long.
Flying along clifftops
into the clouds that break their hue like gods,
teasing them into stories. My mind breathes
deep, penetrating breaths until I remember

that I am more than me, and this symphony weaves its complex waves of sound and
thought and I could weep with relief because this moment is me and my mind—
and I—I can breathe freely until

   —the cat mewls—
          —the oven bleats—
                   —the doorbell chimes its final countdown—

     and I am once again no more than I am supposed to be.

MICHELLE PENN

## The Water-Reader

Water is a language you have to know by
feel. There is no Rosetta Stone, no
compendium of grammar. Every text
changes before you can discern the meaning
and every meaning is slippery. It glides over
your body, deciphering you much more
thoroughly than you decipher it. Some
water steams and burns as you try to grasp
its message; some hardens to ice, obscuring
anything at all legible; some is playful or
cruel: foam flicking from waves, storm-silt
that blurs clarity while you stand knee-deep,
trying to snatch sound or significance. A
puddle should be easier but it's not. You can
stare at it for hours, yet all you see is
pavement, bottle caps and cigarettes stubs
—if you're lucky, a reflection of the sun.

———————

No one should ever interrupt when someone is saying something difficult—

———————

I am constantly overlooked. My life
        is spent straining to the burbles and trickles
of rivulets, the clatter of waves
        on shingle and especially the diaphanous notes of mist. When I
kneel beside the fountain of a
        ruptured water main, the ignorant think I'm just drinking.
The most difficult moments are
        when I perspire and risk contaminating a text. And what if,
heaven forbid, a tear drips
        into a pond where I'm working? For that reason, I have
renounced emotion. Reading water
        requires acuity of vision, speed of intellect, a keen ear.
Most people believe water is without speech—
        not the first of the dangerous mistakes they make, and often.

IAIN TWIDDY

# The Sting

That was the winter when night upon night
he'd scuffle and wriggle his way from the bush,
padding the frost like a shower of glass
as the air bristled. Then he'd dip his pinched neb

to the lip of the milk the cat's weaving
eased out, below where the webs of our breath
pinned from the pane; he'd snuff it like a rose
leaning out fully, and set our blood quivering.

That was until–the lilac silent, composed
as before, the stars shattering the grass—
we kneeled so long on the chairs, so frozen and shushed,
it felt like the needles would never retreat.

# Leasgill

Through the fence swept a morning of horse breath,
the squelch and squeak of dew glossing sprawl-grass,
the Kent churning mere-water and sheep-scut.
Under oak-shoulders, on the low slopes, we tracked
autumn buds, and words like *lush*, *gill*, and *spore*.
Put your thumb to the nub, she told me, and pluck.

I look back at the spoors of my damped shoes,
then along raggy bramble lanes to a house
that clings to the hill-bank. Bed was *downstairs*.
Mould-snug, I wormed and worried if the ceiling
fell, how long it would take to emerge, for air
to burst through the dirt; as I fret openly now,
lest some day the memory can't reach deep enough,
can't plant me back in its rich and strange ground.

# DOMINIC BOND

## When it Snowed

I ignored your plea for gloves,
skin cracking like ice down
a hillside. You drove us home,

the radio broadcasting
news to your dismay,
someone getting something

they shouldn't. Once home,
I left mud on the floor
so felt the back of your

hand, after which you shared
out tea and biscuits. Now
you're gone, the hands of

summers building sandcastles
or holding my bike upright
stand out in each picture,

like you,
sometimes muslin,
sometimes birch.

# Minster

A tired crucifix hangs on
to a building looking uncertain

of its place amongst
Hornbeam trees whose boughs

are as grand
as was imagined.

Some words remain
in stone that's overwhelmed

by moss, fighting to be heard.
An old face maintains order,

unperturbed by absence,
protected in a membrane

guarding the scene.
He is of a handful

that have stood still,
seraphs of defiance.

LUKE BEDDOW

# The Death of Robin Hood

No-one can know the things he might have said
if left alone to rage against the static,
fighting at the borders of his wavelength;
voice carried on magnetic storms
through burnt-out monoliths of steel.

Yeoman, rebel, anarchist,
leafy face in weathered stone.

Light shines green through panes of oak.
*Lay my bones where this shot lands.*
An arrow falls from slackened string,
a council seat is lost to nationalists,
a wormwood star is seen above the Severn.

JEAN ATKIN

## Chorley Flat Iron Market

Whoever counted the width of cloth
in cubits, elbow point to fingertip,
sang her years over flick and slam
of shuttles down the mill.

The dark tarp drips all Lancashire
upon us, while she shouts, 'Feel
that, luv,' then tips a bolt of cloth
along the stall for us to touch.

She points to where the pattern doesn't
quite align at the repeat. She talks
fast dye, raw cotton fluff and fustians.
Ma strikes her deal in shillings.

The sale is measured out, the cotton taut
from outstretched hand to nose
in quickly counted yards. The cloth stall lady
wears three jumpers and a flowered apron.

Ma says she's loud because she's deaf:
two decades in the weaving shed,
lip-reading consort to King Cotton's final days,
working out her shifts for that bright thread.

## GILL McEVOY

### Snowdrop Woods

The ground is dry. Mid-November,
no sign of them now.

But months ago, after weeks of rain
so heavy the paths were turned
to boot-wrenching mud,
I saw them.

They swarmed up every bank,
crammed every hidden hollow,
smothered the edges of the path
and lit the river's bank.

I found myself snow-blind
in their blizzard of white,
and I forgot the mud.

# Beneath Three Sycamores

Eight or so sheep, three of them this year's lambs,
are cushioned on this wind-blown Yorkshire hill,
feeling the earth's warmth through their fleece.

Ten yards away, side-up in the sun, another lies,
the jelly of its eyes plucked out
by the pin of a crow's sharp beak,
its scrags a concentrated buzz of flies.

Beneath the trees the resting sheep are folded close.
Their low bleats hold no keening note;
they sit there, sliding their jaws from side to side,
stare at nothing through their yellow, glassy eyes.

# EMMA HARDING

## The Watcher

I will build myself a hide in the woods,
creep there at dawn with a tartan flask
and wait for them, my lost ones.

At the start, each will come alone,
gusted sudden upon a clearing,
lifting their nose to sniff the air.

Even in shadow I shall know them
by the tremor of their outline,
the particular pulse of their leaf-tread.

Soon they'll come in twos and threes,
stumble laughing into view,
arms draped around shoulders,

younger than when we last met,
eyes watered with the day's promise,
speaking in tongues I can't translate.

The fisher trees loosen their nets
to shake them into being—the lost
who are dead and the lost who are living.

ZOHAR ATKINS

# This Is Just to Say
*after William Carlos Williams*

I have eaten
the gods
that you left
in the Middle Ages

and were probably
saving
for Pesach

Forgive me
they were so cold
and heretical

# Miranda Lynn Barnes

## Three Poems *from* 'Twelve Foundation Stones of the New Heaven'

*Foundation Stone Three*
### Chalcedony: Orion Nebula's Trapezium Cluster

Fog thicker than Brigadoon. It's a no-place place, the world inside a lowered cloud. I have no idea where I'm going, yet my feet press over solid ground and I keep walking. The musk of winter days that see no sun. Shapes darken, emerge in and out through layers of milky graphite mist. My eyes tell me they are there, but each figure disappears in cool softness when interrogated by my touch.

Grey swirls curl across the bright lights ahead. A waxy luminescence. What do they obscure? A deep black hole could be at the centre of this, at the centre of all things; I could fall through and through, down and down. What glows bright is never what it seems to be. Yet I arrive at the entrance where I find you.

What we do in secret. When we close the door. We hunt for each other through the darkness that is thick as fog, fools we are, the dark is soft like ashes cooled between the fingers. We hope for winter rains that will clear our sight. Bursts of light, revealed by the reflections in our eyes, reflections of the divine. We could speak by silence, we could fall and fall.

*Can you loose Orion's belt?*
I can. Close the door.

*Foundation Stone Eight*
## Beryl (Aquamarine): Neptune's Hemispheres

This will be the third time I nearly drown.

As if I am suspended in a seawater marble, ripples of paler light iridesce under and over me. Time is garbled. That's how I ended up here, the compass and the clock both washed clean. From the top of the diving board, into the pool, everything was cool and turquoise. After the splash I was liquid and weightless, there was no top nor bottom to the sphere, all was chlorine blue.

Down I went, and spun an orbit underwater. Now, up I aim to find only more down. The teal, hard tiles of the bottom throw me wild into dissonant gravity—this should be surface, permeable, leading to air. Tossed by my own flailing, I am spinning dark against the water, like a storm contains me. I cannot see through the swirls. My lungs sing with pain.

Another splash, a hook of arm, a swift pull and I see clear, breathe out the blue-green sting of fear.

*Foundation Stone Nine*
## Peridot: Planetary Nebula NGC 6210

I came to them for strength, and they took me to the trees. Three days in a northern state, my two best friends like brothers wasted no time: reminded me of sunlight in a forest, a world of better lovers.

We parked and walked through every pathway circling the arboretum. The sun beamed down around us until it seemed to glow inside of each countless leaf and blade of grass, haloed every person we saw walking on these paths. A cluster of women draped in scarves lingered far ahead, their head-clothes billowing and gleaming like stellar winds in magnetic fields

Once more around, another loop, a car ride through trees at their most fluorescent, warm radiance expanding through the canopy. We had a song to carry with us, made of burr oak and sugar maple, of goldenrod and bird's-foot trefoil, of fox sedge and bergamot, of the hands of friends and leaving all that need be forgotten.

The more of my sorrow I shed there, the greener my heart became.

# *Note*

The poems presented here are from a series entitled *Twelve Foundation Stones of the New Heaven*, which is part of a yet to be published poetry collection of the same name. The series explores how poetry functions as a place of dialogue between science and spirituality, via the lens of human experience.

I envisioned each poem as being composed of a 'braid' with three strands. The first strand was to assign a 'foundation stone' from Chapter 21 of the Book of Revelation. Verses 19-21 detail the author's prophetic vision, where he is shown the creation of a 'new heaven and a new earth' by an angel. Twelve gemstones adorn each corresponding foundation of this new holy place, above which sits a 'city of gold, pure as glass.'

As someone raised in the Christian tradition, but for whom its limitations became a heartrending constriction, I sought out ways of incorporating the awe and precision of science into my own new vision for spirituality. For me, these things could not be separated or limited by any pre-existing doctrine. I took material from religion and reframed it in a cosmic sense, but also embraced the significance of personal experience through my use of subject matter and description.

For the second strand of each poem's braid, I used images of astronomical phenomena taken by the Hubble Space Telescope as a primary resource. I searched for images that shared each particular gemstone's various physical characteristics: colour, clarity, lustre, how they interact with light. The selected astronomical image made up the final part of each poem's title

The final strand of the braid was to select an experience to explore that could be evoked using descriptive language and that would also describe both the foundation stone and the cosmic image. The selected experiences were significant, spiritual, of great *soul-depth*, but also ones that I felt would be unexpected.

*Miranda Lynn Barnes*

# Max Mulgrew

## Arrival

After all, you're newly arrived and are hurt
and confused as if you'd been caught
swearing aloud in the high street church,
or peeing up its Gothic revivalist door—
so we'll go in and hold hands in the pews
until you're convinced you've broken no laws.
We'll avoid the graffiti and burnt-out shops
as we search in the dark for the evening star.

After all, you're newly arrived and are far
from where your alignment became flawed.
You need sky and rocks, the perpendicular,
a plumb-line, a steeple with bell-ropes
and a tether fastened firmly to Earth's core,
because now you're here, I need to be sure.

ANGELA T. CARR

## Paper Fish Balloon

Once, I dreamt Viggo Mortensen gave me a paper fish balloon—
a Betta, a Siamese fighting fish, an onionskin tantrum
of snowy fins. I grasped its waxed red string in my fist
and woke, something of its bubble of joy
hovering intact, until my wits pricked
and it burst or swam into the dim
undercurrent of morning.

Every so often,
the figment loops
and returns
(the joy too)
in the weightless,
iridescent blink
past sleep,
and I come to,
empty-palmed—
*I do not try to catch it—*
my fingers,
open, unstrung,
gifting flight,
gifting the sea.

# GARETH CULSHAW

## Conwy Castle

The stones held each other above the town.
Arrow slits in the walls told me the sea
was out there being dragged back by the moon.

The turrets allowed steps to twist inside them.
My whole foot was able to step on each rise.
Father followed as the sun anchored his lungs.

I put my head between the merlons, peered
through the embrasure, and looked at rooftops,
roads, people, gulls and a world I did not see

when I was down there. Then father reached
the top and his breathing pulled me away.
When he looked he saw the sky and told me

Ireland was at the end of his finger. My eyes
widened at another country's name. He told me
about other places, mapped the earth for me

before I went to secondary school. When we
got home I heard him tell mum the rooms
of the house and where things went.

But I hadn't realised she already knew.

# Before Al Zab His Name Was Adam

He wears shoes that are a size too small.
Struggles to carry shopping home
because of his hernia.

His wife left him years ago, ran off with a postie.
They now deliver letters. She does the odd
numbers and he does the even.

He talks about the seventies like it's the nineties
until his neighbour closes the windows on him.
Then he walks up and down the garden

whistles songs that play in his head.
He stretches his washing across two lines
so the garden looks to have a tent three days a week.

From behind, his neck seems to be giving birth
to an egg. His moustache is nicked from a cloud
that he once walked under when drunk.

He has war medals on his wall. Shivers
nightmares at three am. Rumour has it he was lost
in Al Zab for two days.

To survive he ate the fingers of a dead soldier.
When the back-up team arrived they saw him curled
up like a dog behind a hedge.

On the drive out of there he picked out
a fingernail from between his teeth. Told his officer
he had left his name behind.

# George Aird

## Gallery

My insides on the light box
while I am asked to undress: my body pale
and whole, smelling of sun cream and stale
deodorant. It is summer, the ground is hard
and everywhere boys are injuring themselves in sacrifice.
The doctor has seen it all before,
the blue of my exit, a clavicle stalled and open like a bridge.
He tells my mother not to be alarmed by the bruising,
the dark reservoir, accidental and stagnant,
pooling across my neck and shoulder.
The mother, who has watched boys die on Sunday mornings,
who is haunted by darling familiars,
holds the cold thing tight to her chest.
The map is close enough to the memory.
A man's body is bloodproof, after all.

*

Years later, it is raining and we find ourselves idling
around a Rodney Graham exhibition in the old Mill.
Maybe it is something about the way we remember ourselves,
always in an eye of brilliant light, always undressed for photographs,
or perhaps it is because this body has grown used
to examination, just as a much-loved book will eventually
forgo its order. The wall becomes the size of a portrait,
or a mirror, while I clutch the old injury like a string of pearls.
You say, I am always looking for detail. Looking for an invitation.
I am a boy delighted, panicking at the threshold of my skin.

# Marc Brightside

## The Fine Day

When Christopher went up in flames,
it was like a picture from a movie.

All his closest friends were there,
though neither were on time,
and his pension money paid for
the most simple service possible;
coffin closed in Putney Vale,
riding on a spark. Three months,
he'd waited, steady as a hornet,
silent as a pyroclastic dome.

I took the roundabout way home,
wrapped in distance and guitars
as dead leaves tangoed in the wind
and summer peeked through autumn's
dressing gown. I smiled, somewhat.
And the young lady with the pugs,
eyes like flying saucers, paws like
leather lily pads, she smiled too.

There was Wi-Fi on the train,
a symphonic air conditioner,
and Mr Backwards Baseball Cap
wrote poetry across from me:
something about watercress,
something about coffee beans.
I bought a steak and stilton pasty
without looking at the price first,
and every set of crossing paths
turned green for my departure.

And as I stood before that house,
I knew the past was ending for me,
a quarter-orbital rotation settled,
done, splintered in a heartbeat,
in an echo, in a cheapo immolation.

After Dad went up in flames,
I called him Dad, again.
And everything was fine.

JAMES GIDDINGS

## Alternative talks in alternative timelines #15

My mother and I are sat on the sofa in the living room
like two people taking the name of the room
seriously, both of us breathing as if breathing were infinite,
as if we weren't a simple mess of cells capable of death
and longing. She is angling her body towards mine
so we are more face-to-face than side-to-side
which, in the movies, tells me she has something
uncomfortable to say. Her hands play dead in her lap
and the room sighs all its warmth out.
Soon she will recall the story about how my hamster
ran away, her face empty as a cage when she says
dad too has gone and won't be around the house as much.
After, I will drink my half-glass of lemonade, walk up
to my blue bedroom, saying, *gone doesn't mean dead,*
*doesn't mean dead,*
*doesn't mean*
*dead.*

SNEHA SUBRAMANIAN KANTA

# To say goodbye one last time to those you love

Stand on the edge of a high cliff
& fasten a harness on your waist

unbuckle the landscape, feel the
warm escape your skin in parts.

Hold a piece of your favourite fruit
in between the roof of your mouth

& the tongue. Imagine a deer run
away from a predator lynx & exhale

the same sigh of immediacy, as if
your heart is in your mouth & you

leap fast & speak truths. Admit
fear & un-belong as the deer runs

deeper into an unknown forest. Say
there will always be yellow leaves &

a river, that the leaves will be a wreath
of sun & the river, a moon with scales.

Undo the body, the weight of the world
on your shoulders & reach for the blue

sky upon which your body is a foamy,
white cloud, unaware as it fleets, vanishes.

Practice descent with an open mouth to keep
an exit gateway for consciousness to escape

& utter the name of your beloved as life flashes
before your open eyes, downslope, then gone.

Embrace the otherness of your un-being, how
it lets go. The gilded day. The freefall.

# GERALDINE CLARKSON

## All Souls' Day, Masham

*and Autumn has been gashing herself in the gardens early,*
*her gammy leg suppurating crimson in the hedgerows,*
*splashing Japanese Maples and dragon trees, and depositing sick orange*
*onto copper beeches, as she limps and wobbles to winter. In her uncertain progress*
*she hauls down horse chestnuts whose burnt hearts show behind spiky plackarts—*
*sick with armour. A thin silver dolour winds through the season.*

November 2nd, and I am back at the grave,
still risen like a dowager's hump, unrepentant.
I leave red geraniums.

There is a goat's broth of a gathering afterwards,
the passing round of soupy condolences.
A shadowy man in a maroon velvet jacket
and tap dancer's shoes, stirs spices into a tureen.
'We could have a song now, in honour …' he says,
looking at me. I demur, putting a hand to my throat
where, I've forgotten, I'm still wearing her choker.
He hands out individual pork pies, like recriminations.

The Heaven Ladies come in after late shift, pulling off beanies
and letting shot-silk blue hair tumble. One of them calls me over
and gives me some forms, everything to be completed in turquoise.
'There's no rush,' she says, 'only they're always switching rooms
and it will be less confusing—' (someone hands her a glass of mulled purple)
'—if you do it before midnight.'

The print doggy-paddles in front of my eyes,
*wheretofore*s and *whereunto*s and *notwithstanding*s coagulating
like raisins in cake. 'I'm not sure,' I begin, but they've all turned away
to where someone has started up on the piano, and is serving low curves of jazz.
'And don't forget the wax seal!' one lady spits back
through the gristle of a pie she's chomping. Someone phones

from the hospital to say there's been a mistake, no-one
has died, and the funeral is thereby declared invalid, if not
actually illegal. The words are bluebottles circling the room,
causing outrage and sniping. The maroon-tapdanceman
seems to hold me personally responsible and says he'll be in touch
for expenses. The Heaven Ladies ~~suppress little sighs and~~ smile
maternally, buttoning themselves up against the east wind
and calling out *seeyousoon*s.

As they depart, I stand in the doorway like a broken sheep.
I say, 'You are welcome,' but am careful not to let my hand stray
too far from the latch.

## CLAIRE WALKER

## When She Makes Apple Pie with Her Mother

The apples start to wither
at the interrogation of flames,
she recalls that first time she noticed
a chink in the completeness of home.
The harvest over, the apples fallen,
she remembers how she ran through trees,
branches shading ground in conspiracy.
She sees herself dropping to her knees
and gathering the fruit.
The texture sticks with her—
a writhe of maggots across her hands,
the spoiled flesh giving way to pulp,
brown and sticky and rancid.
She learned that perfection rots,
the beauty, the moment, gone.


The beauty, the moment, gone.
She learned that perfection rots,
brown and sticky and rancid.
The spoiled flesh giving way to pulp,
a writhe of maggots across her hands—
the texture sticks with her.
And gathering the fruit
she sees herself dropping to her knees,
branches shading ground in conspiracy.
She remembers how she ran through trees,
the harvest over; the apple fallen.
A chink in the completeness of home:
she recalls that first time she noticed,
at the interrogation of flames,
the apples start to wither.

## Zannah Kearns

## He Stopped

One time, my dad & I
were in a car crash.

He slammed the breaks &
a car smashed into our backs.

Exploding heart-shock
of collision—shunted in our seats,

breath jolted
from our chests.

Silence
falling around us,

like the ash petals
of a bonfire.

My dad
getting out of the car,

walking
to the other driver,

saying—
*I'm sorry.*

*There were birds, you see.*
*Sparrows.*

He stopped
because sparrows

were hopping
in the road

& because his daughter
sat beside him.

The heart in my child chest
beat at such courage—

admitting stopping
for birds.

## Matt Bryden

## Apple

Slice it thinly as you like—
as thin as tissue—
and lay it over the eye;

the knife, sharp enough
not to be felt as it tops and tails,
severs shadow.

This one sensation:
the lightness and wet

and then the tang and tine-stir
that make of an area of skin
a tattoo; a nib, a flywheel.

*

Baize tables, up a flight, visible from the paving—
we speculate for a number 36

and you there leaning into the wind
with a ripening of the shoulders

tell me you worked here
before a change of manager,

ran tables, sweated 240 calories an evening
and came home filled with light

before your closed eyes gave dictation—

your cedar notebook scattered with pips,
fingers pressed to the skyline.

KATE NOAKES

## Dovecotes, burning

The heron perches on ash-green
at the top of the weeping pear.

Pigeons must find another place to coo
their sorrows to the scummy pond.

The cockerel from the lead spire of Notre Dame
was rescued intact, its verdigris untarnished.

Pigeons must find another place from which
to coo their sorrows.

*

Pub terrace: scrunched cellophane from a packet
of cigarettes—the perfect fireball. Acrid smoke

finds a special place in my lungs. Paris stinks
of bonfire, and I don't mean smokers *au terrace*.

# LEE MACKENZIE

## The Tick

I spent a month
trapping beetles
on hills of heather.

In daily brown sweat,
I crushed that heather,
spat at midges near my lips,
pushed decades' moss
down under foot, cut out
rude mouths made malleable
like water dammed. I laid out
my traps until the tick attached.

I'd find her in the shower later,
braving waves of soap growing
as wet minutes passed.

Dressing, I avoided breaking her
carcass. Gingered clothes
round her spot. Her head
in my bloodstream, drinking.

Cut short, she'd vomit
vein routes lead to my heart.
Now, she's growing again,
spilling ink: life's blot.

I will remove her
to avoid bloody troubles—
untie our knot.

I'll watch under the microscope,
her crabby head
screaming beneath a fiddle of legs,
swiping soundless.

I leave it on the slide,
move to the door
until it's a mere dot,
and walk away.

JACK WARREN

## Sonnet for John Milton

When I think of the image we have
of the taciturn, blind, enfeebled puritan,
vehement in his betrayed ideals; awaiting
death or sovereign reprieve, staring
into the darkness of a fire – I like to remember
instead that Milton's father was a musician
who learned his son to sing in consorts,
play the organ and the bass viol—

Then I imagine the great poet
in his last days, not stubbornly repeating
histrionic Latin, planning for the garret
or cursing his physician; but humming
softly with a tired smile, his white eyes
burning—as chorus upon chorus accompanied him.

KATIE HAWORTH

# John Ruskin meets the Medici Venus

After so many years trapped in shy bronze,
the Medici Venus was finally able to move her arms.

Oh, what bliss to raise first left
then right above her head
and flex fingers.
How hilarious
to stand on one leg and hop,
or spin until dizzy.

She wanted to share the joy with her friend, Ruskin,
who had once called her elevated and pure,
and so, arms raised,
breasts, made flesh, meeting gravity
with lopsided collapse
and hair—hair just everywhere—
springing to attention,
a field of prickling bayonets.

'John,' she cried, turning her head to meet his gaze,
'John, just *look* at me!'

Ruskin did not have to answer straight away
because in her excited lope,
she had knocked over a vase of pink roses,
and they stared at them scattered,
spilt water darkening the carpet.

'Shit,' said the Medici Venus.

And because this was not the sort of thing
that Ruskin thought the Medici Venus should say,
he held up one signet-ringed finger and scolded,
'No, no, no.'

He tried to put her back the way she was
and bid her stay put,
but she, so long trapped unfeeling
was tickled by the slightest touch
and giggled without an ounce of divine contrition.

Shoulders squared in medieval hunch,
Ruskin slumped to his desk to revise his opinion
of the piece calling her coarse and inferior
to other Venuses.

Wanting to taste, The Medici Venus
crunched apples from a bowl,
juice running down her pointed chin
and lobbed the cores out the window
at the tattered parasols and passing fashions
ghosting by.

# Tesco Bag

It lands in the graveyard,
arriving on a cold wind.
Grounded, it puffs its feathers,
then opens wings to dance.
Monks play *memento mori*
on metacarpals,
a plague child drums her skull and
a butcher plucks bass
on a cartilage string.
It pirouettes.
White and ephemeral
deadly
albatross you will
outlive them all.

IAN DUDLEY

# The Ironmaster

He has never found a use for beauty
though beauty has use for him.
The scholars wanted a square of light,
a glass roof held up by iron trees.

The trunks, thick leaves and sturdy ribs
were laden with so much wishful
thinking the roof collapsed
in a thunderstorm of glass.

They needed him to finesse
their dreams and be forgotten.
No one wanted to know or care
who he was. A hireling

with nothing of the artist about him,
his name is as unimportant as those
of the craftsmen who arrived in Martignac
like labourers come for the harvest,

or to shovel tar off the reactor roof,
who began their work in the dark
each morning, measuring out their darg
in fresh lime plaster, working while it drank

the paint and light remained, colouring
the blank church with frescoes—Lust, an
easy rider, hanging from the forks of a ram,
Gluttony riding a pig, plump with hunger,

Anger on horseback, the sword sunk
in her breast a pledge of revenge . . .
Paid, they left quietly and without signing
so much as a *pissotière en porcelaine*.

HOWIE GOOD

# Human Beings Against Music

I inhabit a dark little corner. I was five the very first time I saw it. Like every other space I inhabit, it's become utterly cluttered. The upstairs neighbours are loud and obnoxious, and have camels, llamas, and donkeys when the circus is in town. Living and working amid crimes in progress, I'm frequently bombarded by deafening sirens. My work involves a lot of sharp edges and loose ends. Cheating is required. Wherever I find a parking spot, I let children paint on the car. An industrial chimney laced with vines towers above. It heads who knows where from there.

There was a bear and her three cubs outside the door this morning. They followed me to the French Alps and then to Los Angeles. I travel to a lot of places looking for 'trees of significance.' When I find a tree I like, I take its GPS coordinates. That explains being strict about wearing a mask to save my lungs. That explains the piano hidden in a shed nearby. What you don't see is as important as what you do see. Let even more light evaporate. I can work into the night, piano music drifting muffled through the dark.

My gas masks hang on the back of the door. Breathing in the burning flesh isn't a good idea. This is someone's paradise. It's just not mine. The sunlight is harsh and constant. I prefer it to be dim. There's a terrible view of acres of parking lot. I've never seen him, but I hear a stray cat meowing if the windows are open. Hopefully he'll tell me something I don't already know. I've written some thoughts on the wall. They've travelled with me since college. I suppose night would be the last thing. Sometimes I forget it's even there.

# PHILIP MILLER

## Britten at Belsen (July, 1945)

Many bodies burned, and yet here is music:
piano and strings, and the violin's lament
for the ears of the displaced, and the many dead.

Ashes and dust, and underfoot the many dead.
The trees, they do not care, the stone, it does not care
for the music, or this, the breach in nature.

Fingers on bone, pressing for sound, pressing for something.
Menuhin, bent in sorrow, and Benjamin too, bent in sorrow.
Peter, I wish you were here. Would you have the keys?

The key of the Kreutzer Sonata, or the keys to the Roundhouse.
The officer's ball room, where polished leather had circled
in lock-step to Strauss, and the many dead in piles, outside.

In the stone, the fire cooled from Earth's silent birth,
cells contorting to plague, and now this infection
returns, swollen, preparing its killing time again.

Fingers on the bone. And on the taut piano wire hung
notes, sounds in harmony and disharmony, the sweet
lie that there is meaning. Polished leather dancing yet

onto the bus, with the directions to the camp
stamped on its side, in bold legends, and lies
ignored and forgotten, out of human memory.

Thirteen thousands lay, unburied,
when it was found, and in the now
street thugs snigger over Anne and Margot.

Fingers on the many bones, the press of flesh
and tonic and scale, the hum of wood and metal,
hum, humming. Vibration. Sound. Only.

Thugs now dressed as prison guards.
Suits and caps becoming uniforms at the dance.
So will the Risen come swiftly, armed with old memory—

hefting mattocks, remembering the seax?
The polished leather and the circling boots dance.
The leather and the boots, waltzing again.

ALISON BRACKENBURY

# Hope

What will they be, our feeblest ones
who cannot stand?
Swifts who sleep upon the wind,
who never land.

# CAROLINE SMITH

## Cold Files

The man's life has passed in my file.
It's stored away, still open,
just stacked in the filing cabinet,
waiting—for something to change,
a rule, somewhere, in the future.
I lift the dog leg metal arm
and lever back pages to letters
written sixteen years ago,
pleading with the Home Office
to release his passport,
so he could travel to Kabul,
to the bedside of his child
hit by a motorbike.
Five years later, more attempts,
no clear reason,
just a surge of sadness perhaps,
a ruffle of hope
when a chance came to legalise his stay.
The wedge of paper buckles over the rings
and jumps another seven years
to an explosion of requests;
to return home
to reconcile with his dying father.
After that in the file        nothing.

Once I witnessed a raid on a magpie nest.
We'd stopped because of the frenzied
click and clatter of the birds,
suspended vertically, angle brackets
hissing round a tightly bound tree,
a magpie stabbing forays into the thick
woven greenery at a flicker of brown wing.
Then finally, the huge hawk
backing out of the tree
with the dangling fledgling in its claws,
a short futile chase by one of the magpies,
and then afterwards, the silence—
the meadow of wild flowers,
the amplified sound of cicadas,
the magpies        quiet.

## Two Poems *from* 'Men Who Repeat Themselves'

### Men Educating Princes

About war, they say, there is nothing new to drive us mad. It is as common to seek motive in the text, as it is to discover motive in the green room. It is the body in the lake, and by equal turns, the potion in the glass, that may confound the women once more. A man laying down his lance for a room full of books may be haunted by the ghosts of his former lovers, or banished to Lusitania. Two men laying down their lances for a roomful of books may soon realise that silence contains its own peculiar form of danger, or be ready, finally, to read Seneca by candlelight.

## Men Who Own Screwdrivers

Men admire each other's martial arts, particularly during periods of severe economic crises. A dire strait filled with water may be as easily circumnavigated as a dire strait made of jam and holes, but a comma mistaken for a semi-colon may stop up the dam forever and a day. If war is a distinguishing characteristic of human nature, how might we explain the existence of music? If war is a controlled over-reaction to poverty and hurricanes, how might we resist big old men and their annihilations? Men sit down to discuss these matters over dinner with cocaine and strippers. Men may need our help.

JOHN PORTER

## The Council

The dogs have now got in
clawing the dark varnished panels
yapping at gold framed paintings
of dead chairmen with pocket watches.
They sniff for meat in the debating chamber
where remnants of flaking skin remain
still muttering statistics
on how many potholes they've fixed
as outside the light is ridiculous,
and windows start to melt.

## Angel Hangover

I woke with heavy wings
like a limpet witch
dragging my back.
I staggered in circles
a dying bird
in a moonlit carpark,
collapsed on the asphalt
dead river mouth,
memory smashed.

I searched throbbing head
found flashes
of swooping
over centuries of traffic,
angry horns blaring,
then slumped
with a bottle
in a hundred bars
each time confirming,
no one's worth saving.

Behind me, a twitch.
I puke as tattered feathers creak,
haul me to dangle
over pylons and smoke
cold sweat
raining on the world below.

# JOSH ALLSOP

## Sea Wrack

Damocles stumbles from the sparse pine
    at the beachhead down over gravel,
to walk among the fractured limbs of bubbling crab shells,
    necrotic wood giving under his gait.
Granite shards jewelled with coral pock his sandals.

He cups the heavy salt air
    feeling the heft of the collapsing breath
from each waveform spasm.
    Standing on a throne of husks, cowardice expelled from the deep,
it might drag him down, the thought occurs,
    might rend the clothes onto his face choking
him against the briny membrane of his rags,
    cloth valve punctuating his lungs with saline scur.

Uneven stabbing in his heels keeps energy
    stirring restless in his legs, holding him up despite limbs shot through
with lactate and rigour. Disrobing, he exults,
    hoarse breathing; the throat ragged, parched
at the sight of the hulk half-plunged,
    its prow erected from the ice water
some ways out.

He can't cope at the sight of the open sky,
    the way that it endlessly rolls over him,
a tightness in his eyes at the deep colour
    that he is unable to grasp in one single
vision so he looks to the black crests
    gilded with whitewater
lacquering itself on the rock.

Uneasy is the head the sea wrack sits upon,
    his body submerges. The fluid, acrid,
laps against the sores and open wounds recently won,
    forgotten in the torpor of his flight.

The dogs behind are in the trees
    racing down the beachhead,
the thunder of their chords echoing
    off the shore.

No option. The breath is taken lest
    the breath be taken, purgation under rime.
He sinks down suspended in the rippling light,
    contracting his stomach, pulling his navel into his spine
acting as rock.
    Contact. He feels the bones of the bed
and takes small strides at first, lengthening out
    toward the leviathan.

## GREGORY LEADBETTER

## Briar Rose

You've dared yourself to do this:
test flesh on thorn
with nothing to go on
but rumours of bliss
with a woman not dead
but crusted with a curse.
You are not the first
to seek her bed.

Others have come hoping to kiss
the dust from her lips
and wake the kingdom of their desires.
I arrived just this side of her hundred years
and found no throne.
She blossoms through the litter of my bones.

# ALEXANDER VELKY

## Lots

I was harvesting slime with my concubine
    from the quarries down Llangolman way,
when I saw my face in a ditchwater pool.
    My reflection proceeded to say,

'This was not what I wanted from my future.
    This was not how I pictured my lot.
I once had a clear destination in mind,
    but the byways I've somehow forgot.'

So I put my boot through the glass of the pool
    before he could waste more of my time;
but I lost my grip at the rim of the cliff,
    and my boot scuffed and slid on the slime.

I woke in the wet of the quarry's main pit,
    with my toes and my fingertips numb.
A sharp pain in my back like something had slipped,
    and my skin baked to scabs by the sun.

She stood there, up above me, my concubine,
    with the rest of my women and whelps.
I could tell by the look of the lot of them
    there was no use my asking for help.

'Why does the world always feel like it's ending?'
    I whispered. 'It always is,' she said.
And she took my spice, and my rocks and my knife;
    and the lot of them left me for dead.

# Cantre'r Gwaelod: The Ballad of the Sunken Hundred

I climbed the coast to Dinas Head
    one All Fools' evening still
And the *hedd* of that high headland then
    no curlew called to kill.
I stood on the trig-point like a statue,
    my *gorwel* for to see:
Wexford way out to the west of me,
    across the Irish Sea;
To my north, the Llŷn Peninsula
    as clear as Waterford glass,
And all between was the blue waves' sheen,
    as *glas* as new-grown grass.

And it looked like nothing was living down there;
    like nothing ever had:
Like maybe the *gweilgi* was a graveyard sown
    with the ambitions of the mad.
And I fancied I heard a tolling carry
    from the *dwfn* down below
As a black mass landed on the clifftop,
    which I thought to be a crow—
Perhaps a chough? Though its bulk cast doubt;
    and, when it turned, its brutal beak
Was gloomy as *glo*; and croaking, and slow,
    this bird began to speak:

'Foolish man thinks itself apart
    from that which its senses grasp.'
Its voice had no *cerddoriaeth*:
    but a rough and rusty rasp.
A talking bird being nonetheless
    beyond my common ground,
I stared back dumbly at the *cigfran*,
    awaiting another sound.
'Have you nothing to say in your defence?'
    demanded the indignant bird.
I asked myself had I the health
    to *credu* what I had heard.

'It talks to itself, but not to us!'
    the raven shrill declared.
I climbed *lawr* to approach the beast
    But it just stood and stared:
Tilting its head, with an *olewog* eye.
    'Who do you mimic?' I said.
It grunted in gruff disapproval, and shook
    its hangman's hood of a head.
'I speak for *neb* and all others,' it said.
    'But to no end, I fear;
For you men have ears only to hear
    the words you want to hear.'

'Then tell me what you would tell me,' I said.
    'And I promise I'll pay you heed.'
'Promise a *blisgyn* to the ocean floor,'
    it said. 'Just do the deed.
That body of *dwr* you gaze upon
    was our childhood hunting ground.
Among its many fertile fields
    were the choicest morsels found.
Till the *tywysog* of that fair place,
    overdosed with wine,
Guiltless slept as the salt waves crept
    to bury our hundred in brine.'

'A legend,' I said, 'that I've heard before.
    And one that every *gwlad* knows;
A story to worry each child who's born
    where rain falls and wind blows.'
The raven cocked its *pen* and looked
    for a silent moment my way.
'Foolish man thinks tomorrow's safe
    from his deeds of yesterday.'
'What deeds of mine?' I snapped at the bird.
    'Why blame you me for this?'
And on this note from the raven's throat
    came a *swn*, half-laugh, half-hiss:

'This sunken hundred was only one
    of your kin's forsaken lands.
And no *cefngwlad* across these wide islands
    is free from the curse of your hands.'
The *cymylau* gathered above us
    and the sea turned the colour of slate;
A calendar hoping to contain this scene
    could surely display any date.
'Your brain is the size of a walnut,' I told it.
    'I've no such power,' I said.
'No blood nor brine stains these *dwylo* of mine;
    your culprits are centuries dead.'

The bird flapped up at my *gwyneb*,
    before perching itself on the trig;
Shaking its shaggy ruff in a rage
    And grunting like a pig:
'As are the beasts of the forest,' it squawked.
    'And half of the *pysgod* too.
There will be little more than you and yours
    by the time your kind are through.
Only a few *milflwyddiannau* ago
    there were bogs and forests and fens;
Till you came to sow with arrows and bow
    and to lock us in cages and pens;

'You drain the *corsennau* and the marshes,
    lay all the forests low;
Raise silent cells for your mutant beasts,
    reap death wherever you go.'
'But this lowland hundred you lament,'
    I raised a *bys* to its beak.
'Which beast but man could have held back the tide
    And plugged each fresh-sprung leak?'
It snapped the air as I drew back my hand:
    'No need would exist!' it yelled,
'Had your ancestors cared for the *tir* that we shared
    and the ancient oaks they felled.

But you shaved the uplands bald and bare,
    gouged wounds deep into the earth.
Brewed *cas* alchemical poisons to plague
    the mother who blessed you with birth.
You assumed the mantle of mastery
    *dros* all other matter,
And milked the will of the wilderness
    to make your children fatter.
Till to find land capable of feeding your greed
    you had to snatch it back from the sea.
But the *tonnau* wouldn't stand at your command,
    nor leave you be.'

 I glared at the raven and stooped to pick up
    a *carreg* from among the ferns.
'Yes, the sea will still drown you if given the chance,
    and the sun still burns;
And the *gwynt* will still throw down your buildings,'
    continued its maddening rasp;
'And the lightning will strike and the fire will lick …'
    And I felt the cold stone in my grasp.
'And the ice will still freeze all the *gwaed* in your veins
    and the rivers will burst at their banks.
And the soil will cease to reward for your toil,
    no matter your pleas and your thanks—'

I struck the bird cross the side of its skull
    and it flopped, slack to the floor.
The raven had *dim byd* to answer that with,
    so I whispered, 'Nevermore.'
The *nos* was gathering in from the East
    and the sunset was rusty red,
That All Fools' eve as I descended
    the coast from Dinas Head.
And I thought about *Cantre'r Gwaelod* then
    and the flooded lowland's fate:
And when, I wondered, did those of that hundred
    know the hour had grown too late?

## Allwedd – Key

*Welsh words listed in the order they appear.*

*hedd* – peace, tranquility.
*gorwel* – horizon; also, figuratively, the limit of one's mental capacity.
*glas* – blue, blue-green; also fresh or verdant.

*gweilgi* – ocean (archaic/poetic).
*dwfn* – deep.
*glo* – coal or charcoal.

*cerddoriaeth* – music or poetry.
*cigfran* – raven; literally: meatcrow.
*credu* – believe.

*lawr* – down.
*olewog* – oily.
*neb* – no one; or anyone/someone.

*blisgyn* – shard or shell or fragment.
*dwr* – water.
*tywysog* – prince or lord.

*gwlad* – land, as in country.
*pen* – head.
*swn* – sound or noise.

*cefngwlad* – hinterland or countryside; literally: backcountry.
*cymylau* – clouds.
*dwylo* – hands; two hands.

*gwyneb* – face.
*pysgod* – fish (plural).
*milflwyddiannau* – millennia; thousands of years.

*corsennau* – bogs or wetlands.
*bys* – finger or digit.
*tir* – land, as in soil.

*cas* – nasty or hateful.
*dros* – over.
*tonnau* – waves.

*carreg* – rock or stone.
*gwynt* – wind.
*gwaed* – blood.

*dim byd* – nothing; literally: no world, or nothing [in the] world.
*nos* – night.
*Cantre'r Gwaelod* – the Lost Lowland; literally: [the] Hundreddwelling [at] the Bottom. The Atlantis or Lemuria of Welsh mythology. Inundated, according to the story, in the 6th century AD; though science speculates this occurred around 7000 BC.

# Note

Writing poems is like stacking rocks. I don't begin until I've found a foundation stone which begs for others to be stacked on top of it: beautiful, ugly, practical—maybe simply wanting companions. I rarely *make* myself write: I'm lazy. I wait for inspiration; usually a title or a first line. The latter was the case in both these poems. Returning to the analogy, the trick is to keep stacking until it's as big or as beautiful as the foundation will support—and to hope the thing doesn't collapse.

My foundation stones have recently directed me toward first-person narrative poems featuring hubristic men. Many of the big stories of our day, from climate change to social justice, seem to centre such characters; and while it's fair to suggest their stories have been told many times, I try to cast them in a new light. I'm interested in how their minds have been everted, thus having a disproportionate effect on shaping both our natural world and social structures. I'm interested in what these men might see when they look into the mirrors they've fashioned.

'Lots' implies some kind of societal collapse or reversion to a primitive order, and how this grander fate is played out as the lot of one sorry individual, who may or may not invite comparison with the Biblical Lot. 'Cantre'r Gwaelod ...' takes a Welsh myth as a foreboding metaphor. The device of a talking raven was unconsciously borrowed from the Fairport Convention song 'Crazy Man Michael'. Welsh words found their way in because I can't look at (or write about) landscape in Wales without thinking at least partly in Welsh.

Both poems are set in places I've walked my dogs; probably because that's where and when I have time to think. And perhaps that's the reason these poems took shape with mostly regular forms and metres. Glyn Maxwell has written a lot about the rhythms of breath and blood and walking being emulated in poetry, and they're certainly a common factor in my composition. A doctor once told me I had an irregular pulse, so my fondness for recognizable structure in my writing might be a coping mechanism; and maybe the occasional diversions from an established rhythm are reflective of that inner imperfection. I'm not very well schooled on poetic techniques and terminology, but the longer of these poems is a conscious attempt at a ballad, as its title indicates. The shorter poem has a similar but looser arrangement of couplets, and so could be considered a mini-ballad or a broadside.

*Alexander Velky*

**George Aird** is based in the North West of England. His poems have been published in journals including *The North Magazine, The Interpreter's House* and *Under the Radar Magazine*. In 2019, his poetry was shortlisted for the Maírtin Crawford Award.

**Josh Allsop**'s poetry has been featured in *Pif Magazine*. He recently completed an MA in Creative Writing at the University of Birmingham. His PhD, at Durham University, will explore the idea of difficulty in poetry.

**Jean Atkin** is troubadour of the hills for Ledbury Poetry Festival. Her new collection, *How Time is in Fields*, was published earlier this year by Indigo Dreams Publishing.

**Zohar Atkins** is founding director of Etz Hasadeh: A Centre for Existential Torah and is the author of *Unframing Existence* (Palgrave, 2018) and *Nineveh* (Carcanet, 2019), which won an Eric Gregory Award.

**Lynn Barnes** is from the US and now lives in Bristol. She has taught creative writing at Bath Spa University. Her poems have appeared in journals including *New Welsh Reader, Under the Radar*, and *The Interpreter's House*.

**Luke Beddow** lives in Birmingham. He has had poems published in *Under the Radar*. He was an author of collaborative novel writing project, *Circ* (Pigeon Park Press, 2015). He is currently working on a novel about pirates.

**Dominic Bond** lives in London and works for a charity where he supports people with their mental health. His poems have been published in *Driftwood Press* and *Kallisto Gaia*.

**Alison Brackenbury** has won an Eric Gregory Award and a Cholmondeley Award for her poetry, and has frequently been broadcast on BBC Radio 3 and 4. *Gallop*, her Selected Poems, was published in 2019 by Carcanet.

**Marc Brightside** lives in South London. His debut poetry collection is *Keep it in the Family* (Dempsey & Windle Press, 2017). His poems have received commendation in the National Poetry Competition (2016, 2018).

**Matt Bryden** is lives in Somerset where he runs the annual Somerset Young Poets competition. His poem 'Landscape' won the William Soutar Prize in 2019. His books include: *Boxing the Compass* (Templar, 2013) and *The Desire to Sing After Sunset* (Showwe, 2013).

**Angela T. Carr** lives in Dublin. She was winner of the 2018 Laureate's Prize, chosen by Carol Ann Duffy and her work has been placed or shortlisted in over 40 national and international literary competitions.

**Geraldine Clarkson** lives in the West Midlands. Her poems have appeared widely in journals including *Poetry* and *The Poetry Review*. She has won a number of prizes and her second pamphlet, *Dora Incites the Sea-Scribbler to Lament* (Smith | Doorstop Books, 2016), was a Laureate's Choice.

**Gareth Culshaw** lives in Wales. His first collection, *The Miner* (2018), was published by Futurecycle. His second collection, *Shadows of Tryfan*, is forthcoming in 2020.

**Ian Dudley** was born in Dudley. His poems have been published in journals including in *Oxford Poetry*, *The Interpreter's House*, and *The North*. He has won the *Oxonian Review* (2015), *Aesthetica* (2017) and Manchester Cathedral (2018) poetry competitions.

**James Giddings** was born in Johannesburg. His poems have appeared in journals such as *The Poetry Review*, *Ambit* and *Magma*. In 2015, he was awarded a Northern Writers' Award. His debut pamphlet, *Everything is Scripted* (Templar Poetry, 2016), was shortlisted for a Saboteur Award.

**Howie Good**'s most recent collection, *WHAT IT IS AND HOW TO USE IT*, was published by Grey Book Press in 2019.

**Rebecca Ruth Gould** translates from Persian, Russian, and Georgian. Her most recent book is *The Death of Bagrat Zakharych and other Stories* by Vazha-Pshavela (Paper & Ink, 2019). Her poem 'Grocery Shopping' was a finalist for the Luminaire Award for Best Poetry in 2017.

**Emma Harding** is a poet, playwright and radio producer from Birmingham. Her poems have been published in journals including *Poetry Review*, *Magma*, *The North*, *Stand* and *Poetry Salzburg Review*.

**Katie Haworth** is an editor and writer originally from New Zealand who now lives in London. She is the author of four published picture books for children, the most recent of which is *Fearless Mirabelle* (Templar, 2018).

**Leila Howl** recently completed her MA in Creative Writing at Birmingham City University. She writes speculative ficton and poetry that explores intersections between science and literature. She is senior editor at Manaleak. com's MTGUK blog.

**Sneha Subramanian Kanta** is a recipient of The Charles Wallace Fellowship at the University of Stirling (2019). She is editor of *Parentheses Journal*, and reader for Palette Poetry and *Tinderbox Poetry Journal*. Her book *Land: Body / Ocean: Muscle* is forthcoming from Dancing Girl Press.

**Zannah Kearns** is a writer living near Reading. She has an MA in Creative Writing from Cardiff University, and has published a YA novel with Frances Lincoln. She was shortlisted for a TSS flash fiction competition in 2017.

**Faustine Ladeiro-Levent** is a French-Portuguese writer based in Birmingham. She is currently a mentee of Nine Arches Press' DYNAMO scheme.

**Gregory Leadbetter** is author of *The Fetch* (Nine Arches Press, 2016). His book *Coleridge and the Daemonic Imagination* (Palgrave Macmillan, 2011) won the University English Book Prize 2012. He is reader in literature and creative writing at Birmingham City University.

**Lee Mackenzie**'s poems have been published in journals including *New European, Pulp Poets Press,* and *Bonnie's Crew*. He is writer-in-residence at the Josephine Butler College, Durham University and one half of the art collective 'is broken'.

**Gill McEvoy** was winner of the 2015 Michael Marks Award for *The First Telling* (Happenstance Press, 2014). She has two collections from Cinnamon Press and is a Hawthornden Fellow.

**Philip Miller** is a writer and journalist based in Edinburgh. He is the author of two novels *The Blue Horse* (Freight Books, 2015) and *All The Galaxies* (Freight Books, 2017). In May 2019, he was announced as a Robert Louis Stevenson Fellow by the Scottish Book Trust.

**Max Mulgrew** lives in Birmingham. He has worked as a journalist for print, radio and television. He is currently studying for an MA in Creative Writing at Birmingham City University.

**Kate Noakes** lives in London where she acts as a trustee for literature advocacy organisation Spread the Word. Her seventh collection is *The Filthy Quiet* (Parthian, 2019). She reviews poetry for *Poetry London, The North,* and *London Grip*.

**Michelle Penn** is a dual US/UK national based in London. Her debut pamphlet, *Self-portrait as a diviner, failing,* won the 2018 Paper Swans Prize. Her work has appeared in *Shearsman, Magma, Butcher's Dog,* and other journals.

**John Porter** lives in Gloucestershire and has degrees in Russian and Law. His poems have appeared in journals including *The Stinging Fly, Prole, Marble, Atrium* and *Strix*.

**Hilary Robinson** lives in Saddleworth. In 2018 her poems were published in *Some Mothers Do . . .* alongside Rachel Davies and the late Tonia Bevins. Her poem, 'Second Childhood', was shortlisted in the 2016 Yorkmix Poetry Competition.

**Mark Russell**'s publications include *Spearmint & Rescue* (Pindrop, 2016), and *Shopping for Punks* (Hesterglock, 2017). His poems have appeared in journals including *The Scores, The Interpreter's House,* and *Tears in the Fence*.

**Alix Scott-Martin** lives in Rugby where she teaches English & runs writing workshops. She has been published in journals including *Magma* and *Lighthouse*.

**Robert Selby** has had poems and reviews appear in publications including *PN Review, Poetry London*, and *The Times Literary Supplement*. His debut pamphlet was published in 2017, in the Clutag Five Poems series. His debut collection is forthcoming from Shoestring Press in 2020.

**Caroline Smith** lives in Wembley where she works as an immigration and asylum caseworker for a London MP. Her most recent poetry book, *The Immigration Handbook* (Seren Books, 2016), was shortlisted for the Ted Hughes Award.

**Ellora Sutton** lives in rural Hampshire. She was commended in the 2018 Winchester Poetry Prize and recently won the Young Poets Network's Carol Ann Duffy challenge.

**Christina Thatcher** is a creative writing lecturer at Cardiff Metropolitan University and poetry editor for *The Cardiff Review*. Her second collection, *How To Carry Fire*, is forthcoming with Parthian Books in 2020.

**Serena Trowbridge** lives in Worcestershire and is a lecturer of English literature at Birmingham City University. She is author of *My Ladys Soul: The Poetry of Elizabeth Siddall* (Victorian Secrets, 2018).

**Iain Twiddy** studied literature at university, and lived for several years in northern Japan. His poems have been published in *The London Magazine, The Poetry Review, Poetry Ireland Review, The Stinging Fly* and elsewhere.

**Alexander Velky** was born in Birmingham and has spent most of his life in Wales. He has published two short poetry books: *Mistaken for art or rubbish* (Doubtist Books, 2013) and *Rhymes for all times* (Doubtist Books, 2015). His poems have been shortlisted for a number of prizes.

**Claire Walker** is co-editor of Atrium poetry webzine. Her pamphlet, *Somewhere Between Rose and Black* (V. Press, 2017), was shortlisted for a Saboteur Award in 2018. Her third pamphlet, *Collision*, is due in September 2019 from Against the Grain Press.

**Jack Warren** is from Somerset and currently lives in Moscow. His work has appeared in *Corrugated Wave, The Anomaly Literary Journal* and he was recently selected as one of the 'Fifty Best New British and Irish Poets 2018' by Eyewear Publishing.

NOTES

#DearPoetryBrum
@PoetryBrum

POETRY BIRMINGHAM
*Literary Journal*

Printed in Poland
by Amazon Fulfillment
Poland Sp. z o.o., Wrocław

63317469R00061